Turtle Steps of Faith

Navigating Life's Waters With God

Foreword by Cynda Harris

Barbara Pollreis Kleinsorge

Copyright © 2024 by CEO Book Publishing

All rights reserved. No part of this publication may be reproduced, distributed, or transmitted in any form or by any means, including photocopying, recording, or other electronic or mechanical methods, without the prior written permission of the publisher, except in the case of brief quotations embodied in critical reviews and certain other noncommercial uses permitted by copyright law. For permission requests, write to the publisher, addressed "Attention: Permissions Coordinator," via the website below.

info@visionaryglobalmedia.com

www.CEOBookPublishing.com

@VGMC

Ordering Information:

> Quantity sales. Special discounts are available on quantity purchases by corporations, associations, and others. For details, contact the publisher at the address above.

> Orders by U.S. trade bookstores and wholesalers. Please contact Tel: (813) 970-8470 or visit www.CEOBookPublishing.com

Printed in the United States of America First Printing 2024

Bible Scriptures are taken from the New International Version (NIV) and the English Standard Version (ESV)

Artwork (Introduction, page 2): Heidi Haught

Title & Cover deisgn: Madison Kistler

We would like to extend our deepest gratitude to Madison Kistler for her invaluable contributions to this project. Her brilliant ideas and creative vision played a pivotal role in shaping the title and designing the cover of this devotional.

Dedication

First and foremost, this book is dedicated to God. It truly is His book, His message, one of hope and promises. He repeatedly showed me turtles throughout my divorce process, so many times that I began to question, "what's with all of the turtles God?" Because I frequently think in analogies, I began to make connections between that season of my life and the life of a turtle. Believe it or not, we humans have a few things in common with the beautiful sea turtles!

Secondly, I dedicate this book to my wonderful family, of which both of my parents and six of my siblings have all passed away. Four of my brothers passed away during this season of my life. I am blessed to be number twelve of fourteen children. Yes, you read that correctly! I grew up in a large mid-west family that didn't even live on a farm! Our parents gave us a strong foundation of faith to build on and to make our own.

Last, this book is dedicated to my three beautiful children, all grown up now, my daughter in law and my two adorable grandchildren. I love each of you and pray for you every day!

Foreword

Growing up, I often heard the story of the Tortoise and the Hare. It's a simple tale with a profound message: slow and steady wins the race. While the hare's speed and overconfidence led to distractions, the tortoise's deliberate pace and steady focus brought him victory.

What I didn't realize as a child is that this timeless fable would echo back to me in different seasons of my life, offering a valuable life lesson about pace and presence.

In our fast-paced world, it's easy to feel swept away by busyness—chasing goals, keeping up with demands, and filling our days with endless activities and many "to do" lists. But as I've walked through life's twists, turns, and unexpected detours, I've been reminded that this constant rush isn't necessarily the healthiest way to live. Relationships need time to grow; deep connections with God and others flourish in moments of quiet and stillness. Even our personal growth often happens not in leaps but in small, faithful steps.

One of my favorite scriptures, Psalm 46:10, says, *"Be still, and know that I am God."* This simple yet profound invitation calls us to slow down, be present, and notice God's hand at work in our lives. When we embrace stillness and trust His timing, we become more aware of His presence and His guidance, even in seasons of change or uncertainty.

This devotional, *Turtle Steps of Faith*, beautifully captures that call to a slower, more intentional pace. Through its beautiful heartfelt writing, reflective prompts, and space for personal takeaways, it invites you to step off the treadmill of hurried living and into a sacred rhythm of grace and growth.

My prayer for you as you journey through these pages is that you would sense God's direction and embrace His pace. I pray you find joy in the process, trust in the small steps (and pace), and rest in His presence as you move toward the purpose He has for your life.

Take a deep breath, lean into His guidance, and let the journey begin.

Cynda

Introduction

For my devotional inspired by turtles:

Amidst the challenges of my divorce after over three decades together, I found solace in an unexpected symbol: turtles. As these resilient creatures repeatedly crossed my path during the toughest moments, I couldn't ignore the parallels to my faith journey. Join me as I share the profound lessons I learned about resilience, perseverance, and faith through the lens of these steadfast creatures. Just as turtles navigate adversity with unwavering determination, we too can find strength to weather life's storms and emerge on the other side, anchored in faith and peace.

How to use this devotional

1. First, take one turtle step forward every day. Set a time during your day to read the devotional every day. If you are a morning person-read each day of the devotional with your morning coffee, if you can't relate to morning people and are a night owl, then make this devotional and journaling time part of your wind down nighttime routine. Find a quiet space where you can focus without distraction (yes, it's good to unplug). How you start and end your day matters. It is great either way, to start your day with intention and God's word but it is also a peaceful way to end your day, with listing what you are grateful for and going to sleep knowing God has you in the palm of his hand, so you can give it all to him and just rest.

2. You may want a pen, pencil, and a highlighter while reading your devotional too! Each day will have a related scripture, so be sure to have your bible handy... if you don't have one, check out the free YouVersion app!

3. Each day of the month, read that day's **Turtle Talk** and related scripture. Don't forget to look up that scripture in your bible or bible app.

4. Answer the reflection questions.

5 List one, two or even three things that you are thankful for each day. These can be blessings such as feelings, circumstances, people, places or things. This may be a tough season you are walking through right now, but if you got up to see another day, and are able to take another breath, you've already found two things to be grateful for! There was a point in that season of my life where it was truly a stretch for me- I remember writing "I am not thankful for the text I got today... but thankful I have a phone" but the rest of the days were those where I was thankful for a phone call from a sibling or a friend, a kind co-worker, a powerful message I heard at church, another amazing sunrise or sunset, or that just right song on the radio like my favorite station, JoyFM! I have over four years of gratitude journals filled and it is a blessing to be able to look back and see the personal, emotional, spiritual growth and healing in those journals. So many answered prayers! If you get stuck, check out some examples that I wrote during this season of my life. Remember there is no perfect answer and these answers are for your eyes only.

6 Most importantly... once you "learn" more about God's character through reading His word, you "grow" in your faith. Then you'll be ready to "give" that knowledge to others as demonstrated through your actions, words, responses, etc.. You can be the light, right in your very own home, school, work, circle of friends, and network. Be the example of hope, peace, kindness, grace and faith. We are all called to do two things in this life, to love God and to love people. This means ALL people, even our enemies and those who hurt us and we are also called to pray for them. Now that's a whole other level of love to strive for!

The Five Finger Promise

I have lived by what I like to refer to as God's Five Finger Promise. That promise is: "I will never leave thee." One word for each finger (also known as digits) on one hand. Like God promises in Deuteronomy 31:8, He will never leave or forsake us. Anytime that I am stressed, worried, or feeling alone, I tap my thumb to each of my fingers and recite this promise, "I will never leave thee". You don't need anything else, just your hand! Try it, it may help remind you that you are NEVER alone when you walk in faith with God.

Turtle Talk

Like a turtle, don't look back, keep looking forward, keep your eyes focused on God and His promises.

Phil 3:12-14 NIV

¹² Not that I have already obtained all this, or have already arrived at my goal, but I press on to take hold of that for which Christ Jesus took hold of me. ¹³ Brothers and sisters, I do not consider myself yet to have taken hold of it. But one thing I do: Forgetting what is behind and straining toward what is ahead, ¹⁴ I press on toward the goal to win the prize for which God has called me heavenward in Christ Jesus.

Reflection

What in your past is God calling you to let go of?

_____

_____

_____

_____

_____

_____

_____

_____

_____

_____

_____

_____

> Shine brightly. See beauty. Speak kindly. Love truly.
> Give freely. Create joyfully. Live thankfully.
>
> -Mary Davis

Gratitude

"Today I am thankful for a trip
home to spend time with
my siblings and family."

–Barbara

Being Grateful

Write down what you are grateful for today.

Date: _____

1. _____

   _____

   _____

2. _____

   _____

   _____

3. _____

   _____

   _____

Day Two

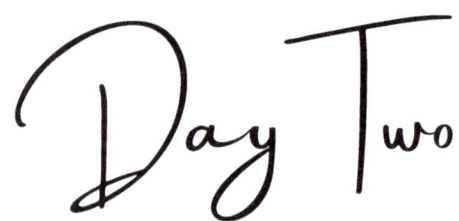

Turtle Talk

Like a turtle, it's ok to retreat back into your shell (safe space), just make it a short visit, not your new address.

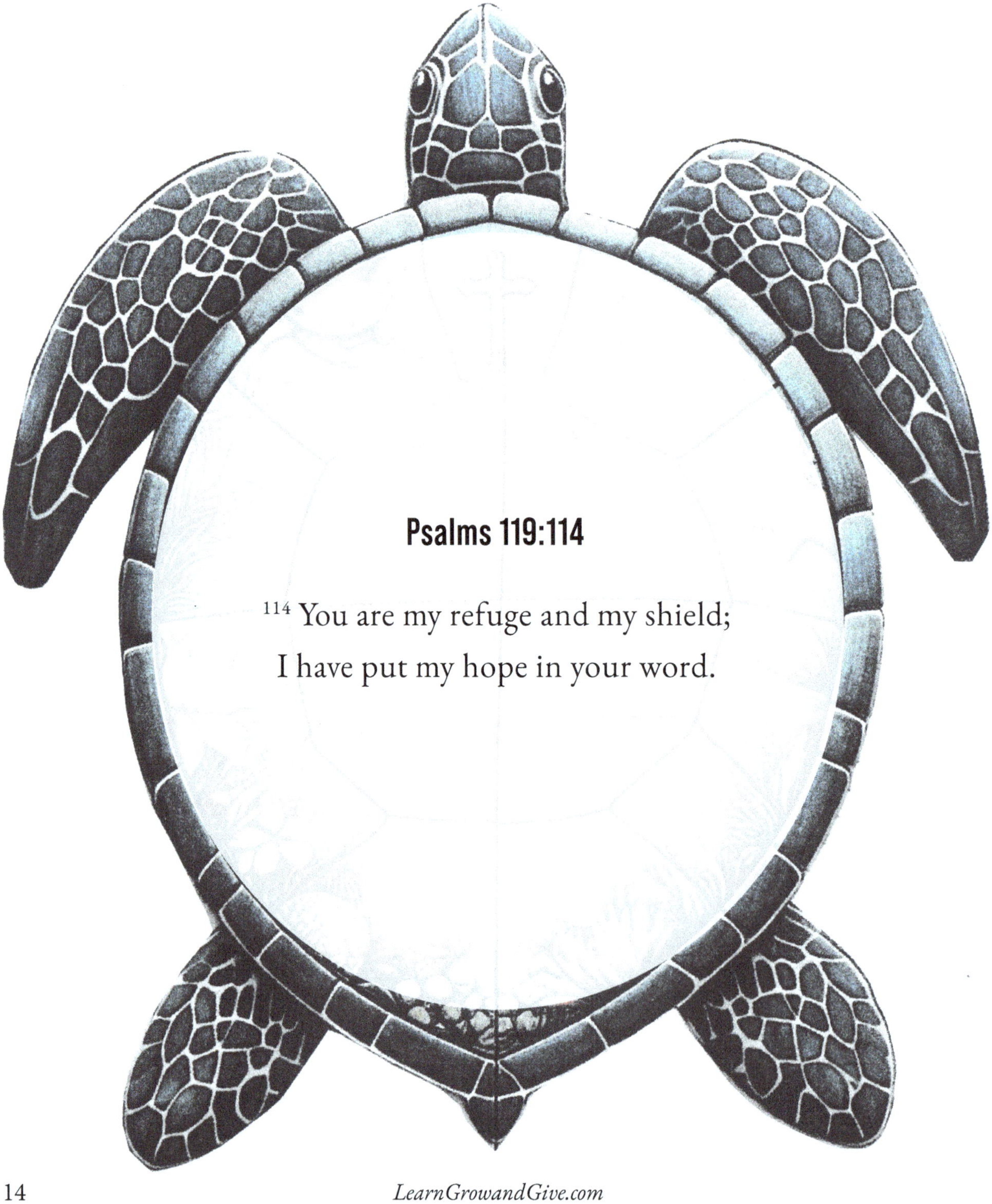

Psalms 119:114

114 You are my refuge and my shield;
I have put my hope in your word.

Reflection

How has God been a source of refuge and rest for you?

> Gratitude is the healthiest of all human emotions.
> The more you express gratitude for what you have,
> the more likely you will have even more to
> express gratitude for.

Gratitude

"Today I am thankful for the weekend
to have time to just rest."

–Barbara

Being Grateful

Write down what you are grateful for today.

Date: _____

1. _____

   _____

   _____

2. _____

   _____

   _____

3. _____

   _____

   _____

Day Three

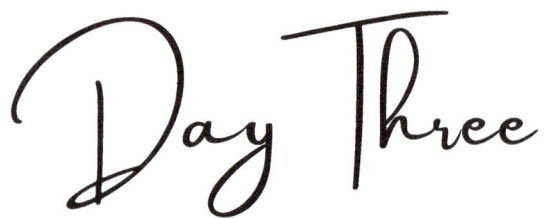

Turtle Talk

Like a turtle, remember you too have a shell for protection to shield you from spiritual defeat. Your shell of protection is the shield of faith, which is part of the Armor of God.

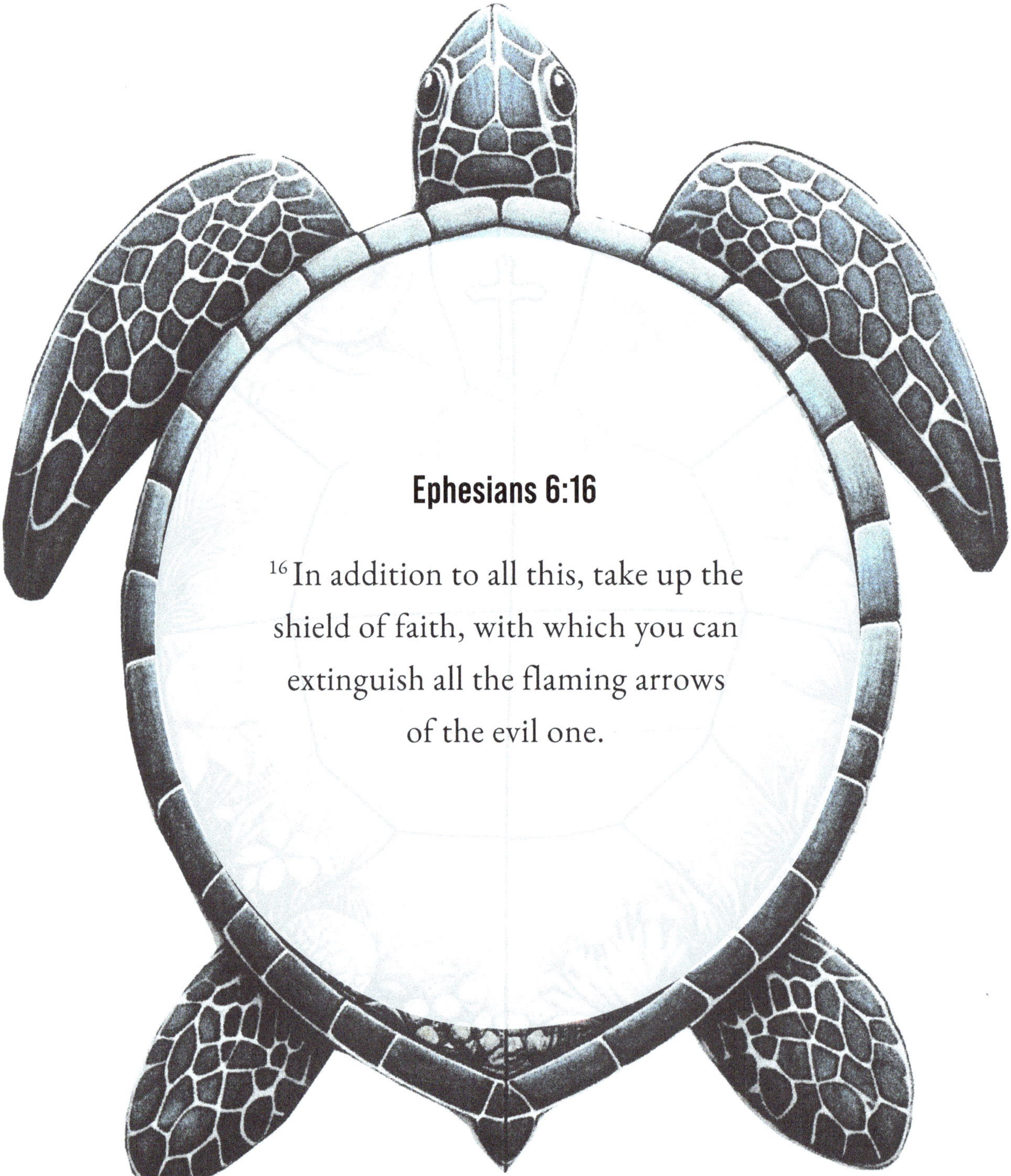

Ephesians 6:16

16 In addition to all this, take up the
shield of faith, with which you can
extinguish all the flaming arrows
of the evil one.

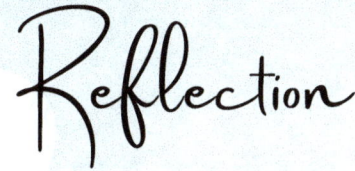

When in your life have you asked God for His protection?

___

> Develop an attitude of gratitude, and give thanks for everything that happens to you, knowing that every step forward is a step toward achieving something bigger and better than your current situation.
>
> -Brian Tracy

Gratitude

"Today I am thankful for God's protection and friends that remind me of His promises."

–Barbara

Being Grateful

Write down what you are grateful for today.

Date: _____

1. _____

_____

_____

2. _____

_____

_____

3. _____

_____

_____

Day Four

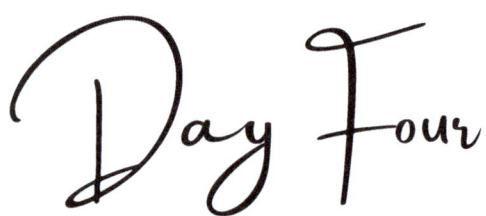

Turtle Talk

Like a turtle, slow and steady wins the race.
Move forward in faith, at your own pace, one step at a time.

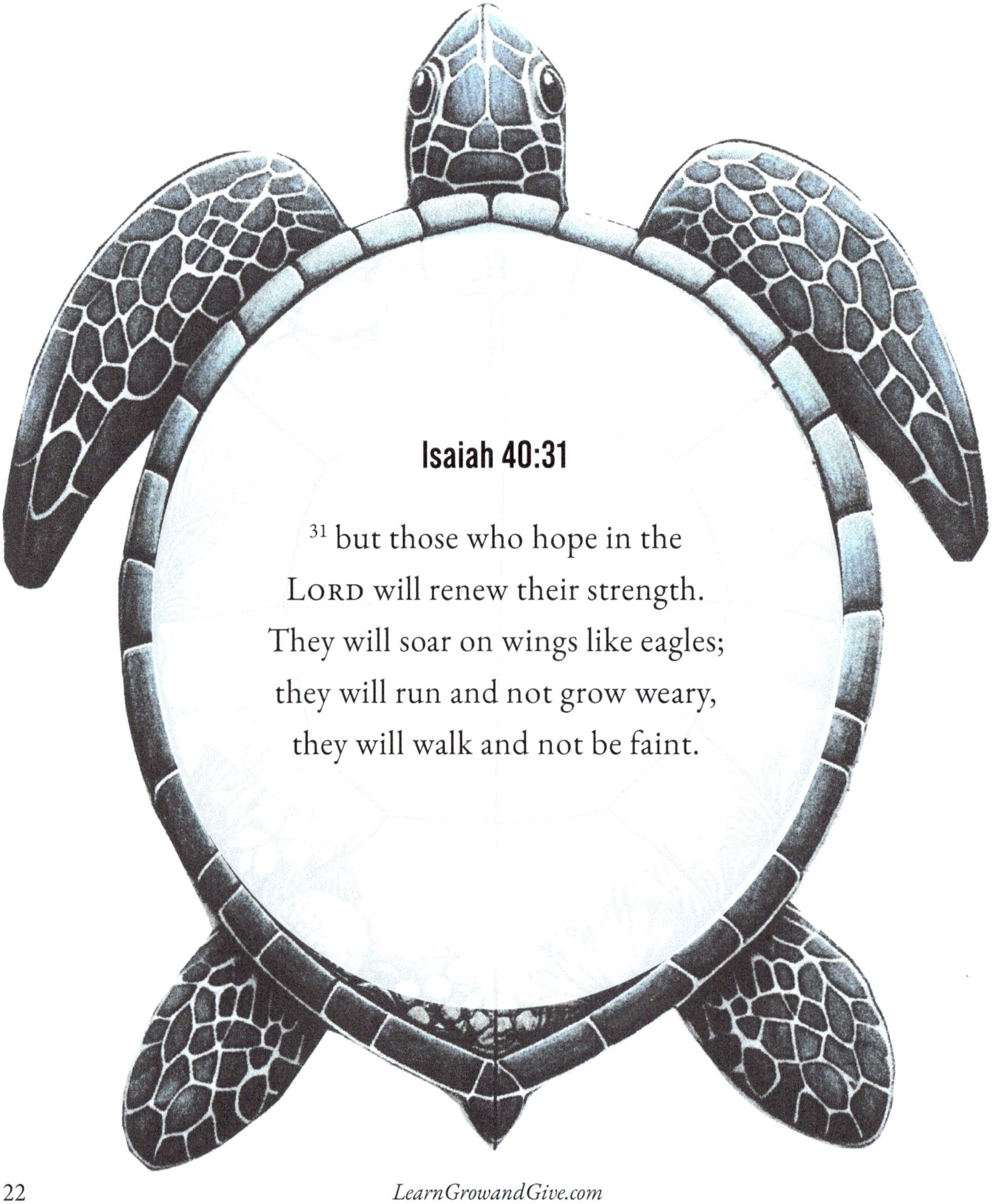

Isaiah 40:31

31 but those who hope in the
LORD will renew their strength.
They will soar on wings like eagles;
they will run and not grow weary,
they will walk and not be faint.

Reflection

How would you help a friend going through a challenging situation using this scripture?

_____
_____
_____
_____
_____
_____
_____
_____
_____
_____
_____

> When I started counting my blessings,
> my whole life turned around.
>
> -Willie Nelson

Gratitude

"Today I am thankful for my children, their hugs mean the world to me and give me strength to keep going."

–Barbara

Being Grateful

Write down what you are grateful for today.

Date: _____

1. _____
   _____
   _____

2. _____
   _____
   _____

3. _____
   _____
   _____

Turtle Talk

Like a turtle has a soft underside, you have a heart. Stay kind, stay true to who you are, who God calls each of us to be. Don't let someone else or a situation make you become bitter or angry. Love God, love people, even your enemies and those who have hurt you.

Matthew 5: 40-43

⁴⁰ And if anyone wants to sue you and take your shirt, hand over your coat as well. ⁴¹ If anyone forces you to go one mile, go with them two miles. ⁴² Give to the one who asks you, and do not turn away from the one who wants to borrow from you.

Reflection

How have you shown kindness to someone else today?

_____

_____

_____

_____

_____

_____

_____

_____

_____

_____

_____

> Gratitude makes sense of our past, brings peace for today, and creates a vision for tomorrow.
>
> -Melody Beattie

Gratitude

"Today I am thankful for the choice we have to choose to respond in kindness rather than out of bitterness or anger. I am thankful for all of those people in my life who have shown me kindness especially when I needed it the most."

–Barbara

Being Grateful

Write down what you are grateful for today.

Date: _____

1. _____

   _____

   _____

2. _____

   _____

   _____

3. _____

   _____

   _____

Turtle Talk

Like a turtle does, it's ok to stop and rest.
Lean into your faith, turning towards God.

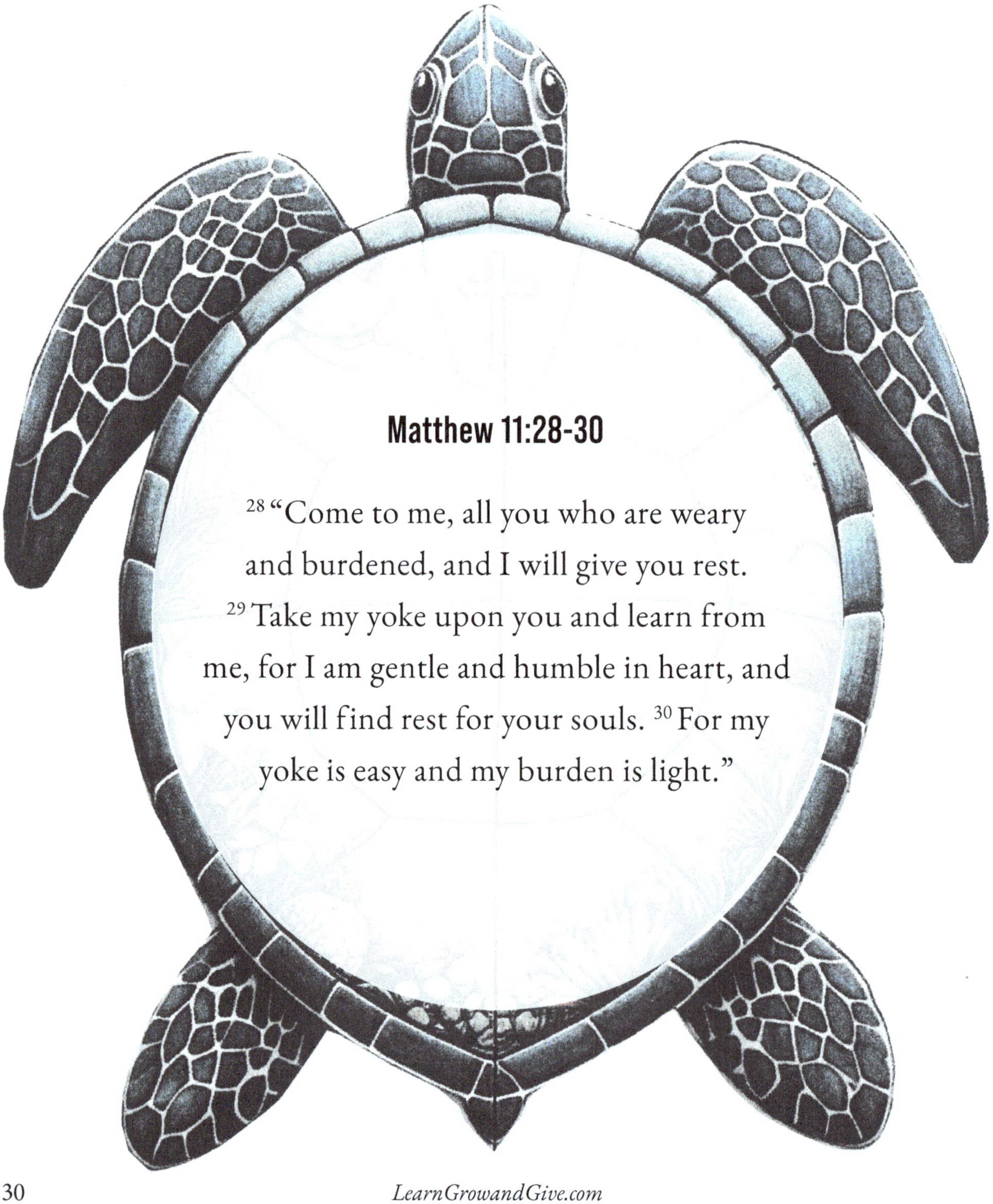

Matthew 11:28-30

[28] "Come to me, all you who are weary and burdened, and I will give you rest. [29] Take my yoke upon you and learn from me, for I am gentle and humble in heart, and you will find rest for your souls. [30] For my yoke is easy and my burden is light."

Reflection

How can you lean into your faith? What is your next right step to take that'll move your story forward?

_____
_____
_____
_____
_____
_____
_____
_____
_____
_____
_____
_____
_____

> "When we focus on our gratitude, the tide of disappointment goes out and the tide of love rushes in.
>
> -Kristin Armstrong

Gratitude

"Today I am thankful for my church and the people that I now call friends. I am thankful to have friends to grow in faith with and be encouraged by."

– Barbara

Being Grateful

Write down what you are grateful for today.

Date: _____

1. _____

   _____

   _____

2. _____

   _____

   _____

3. _____

   _____

   _____

Turtle Talk

Like a turtle, you'll only move forward if you "step" out and try!
Be brave and remember you are never alone. Be Courageous! Be BOLD!

Deuteronomy 31:6-8

⁶ Be strong and courageous. Do not be afraid or terrified because of them, for the Lord your God goes with you; he will never leave you nor forsake you." ⁷ Then Moses summoned Joshua and said to him in the presence of all Israel, "Be strong and courageous, for you must go with this people into the land that the Lord swore to their ancestors to give them, and you must divide it among them as their inheritance. ⁸ The Lord himself goes before you and will be with you; he will never leave you nor forsake you. Do not be afraid; do not be discouraged."

Reflection

When was the last time you did something brave and acted boldly?

_____

_____

_____

_____

_____

_____

_____

_____

_____

_____

_____

_____

_____

> Having kindness, empathy,
> and gratitude every single day.
>
> –Jennifer Aniston

Gratitude

"Today I am thankful to take a walk in nature
and to feel the Florida sunshine on my face."

–Barbara

Being Grateful

Write down what you are grateful for today.

Date: _____

1. _____

   _____

   _____

2. _____

   _____

   _____

3. _____

   _____

   _____

Day Eight

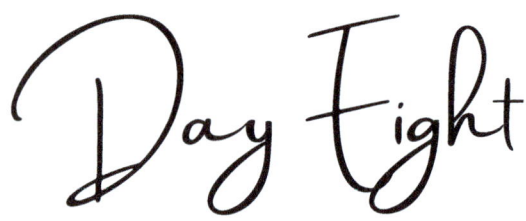

Turtle Talk

Like a turtle, you move and grow, one step and one day at a time – step by step, day by day. Keep going. Have perseverance.

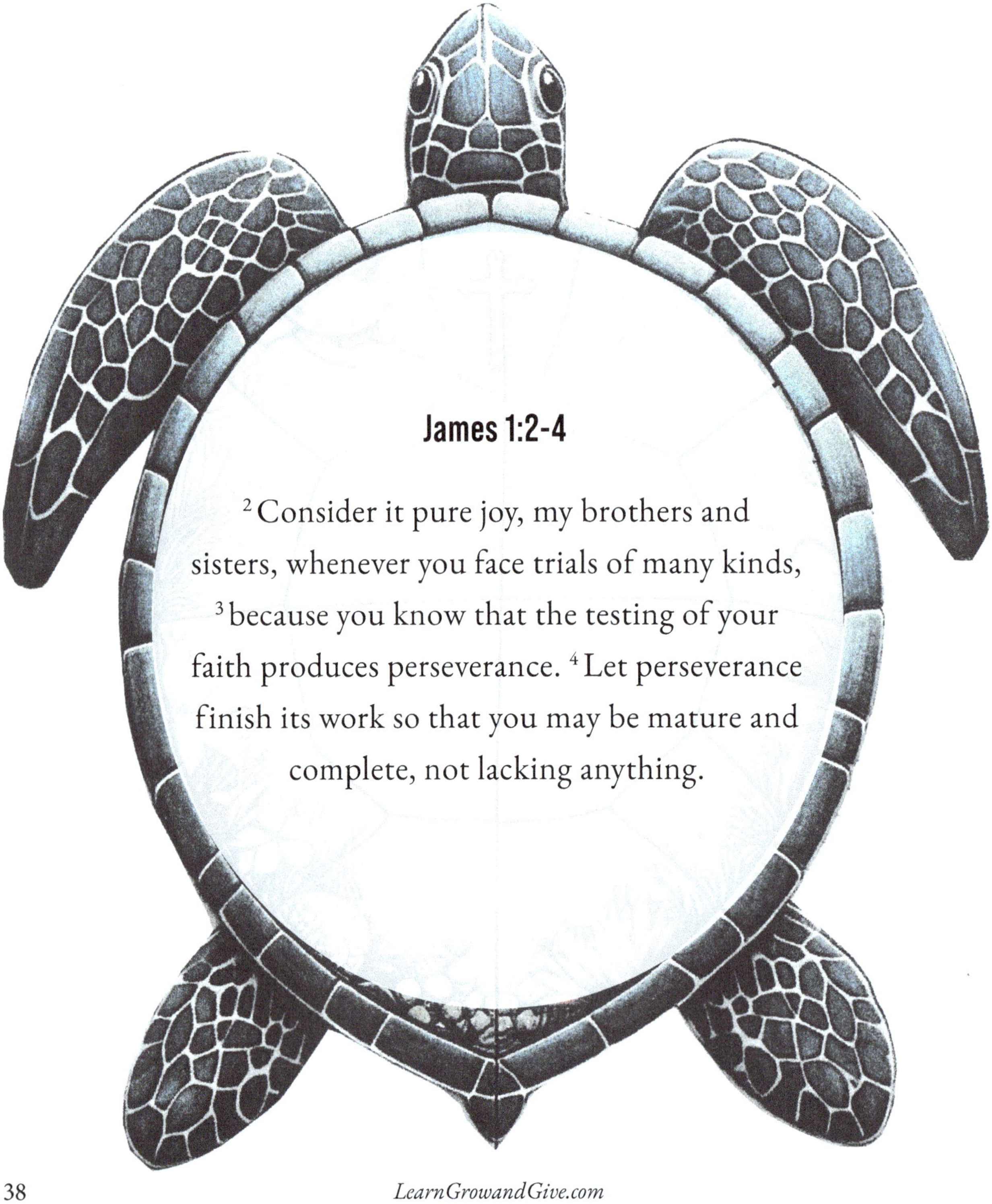

James 1:2-4

2 Consider it pure joy, my brothers and
sisters, whenever you face trials of many kinds,
3 because you know that the testing of your
faith produces perseverance. 4 Let perseverance
finish its work so that you may be mature and
complete, not lacking anything.

Reflection

What is one step you need to take next in your life?

___

> God gave us the gift of life; it is up to us
> to give ourselves the gift of living well.
>
> -Voltaire

Gratitude

"Today I am thankful for having co-workers who are like family, that help to pull you through a tough season, show kindness and grace right when you need it most."

–Barbara

Being Grateful

Write down what you are grateful for today.

Date: _____

1. _____

   _____

   _____

2. _____

   _____

   _____

3. _____

   _____

   _____

Day Nine

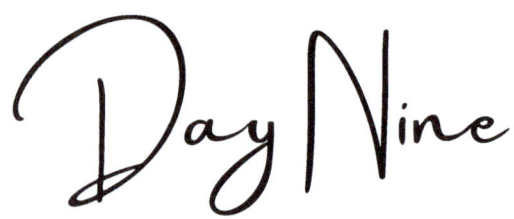

Turtle Talk

Like a turtle, your direction is more important than your speed.
God will lead you in the direction right for you. He will direct your next right step.

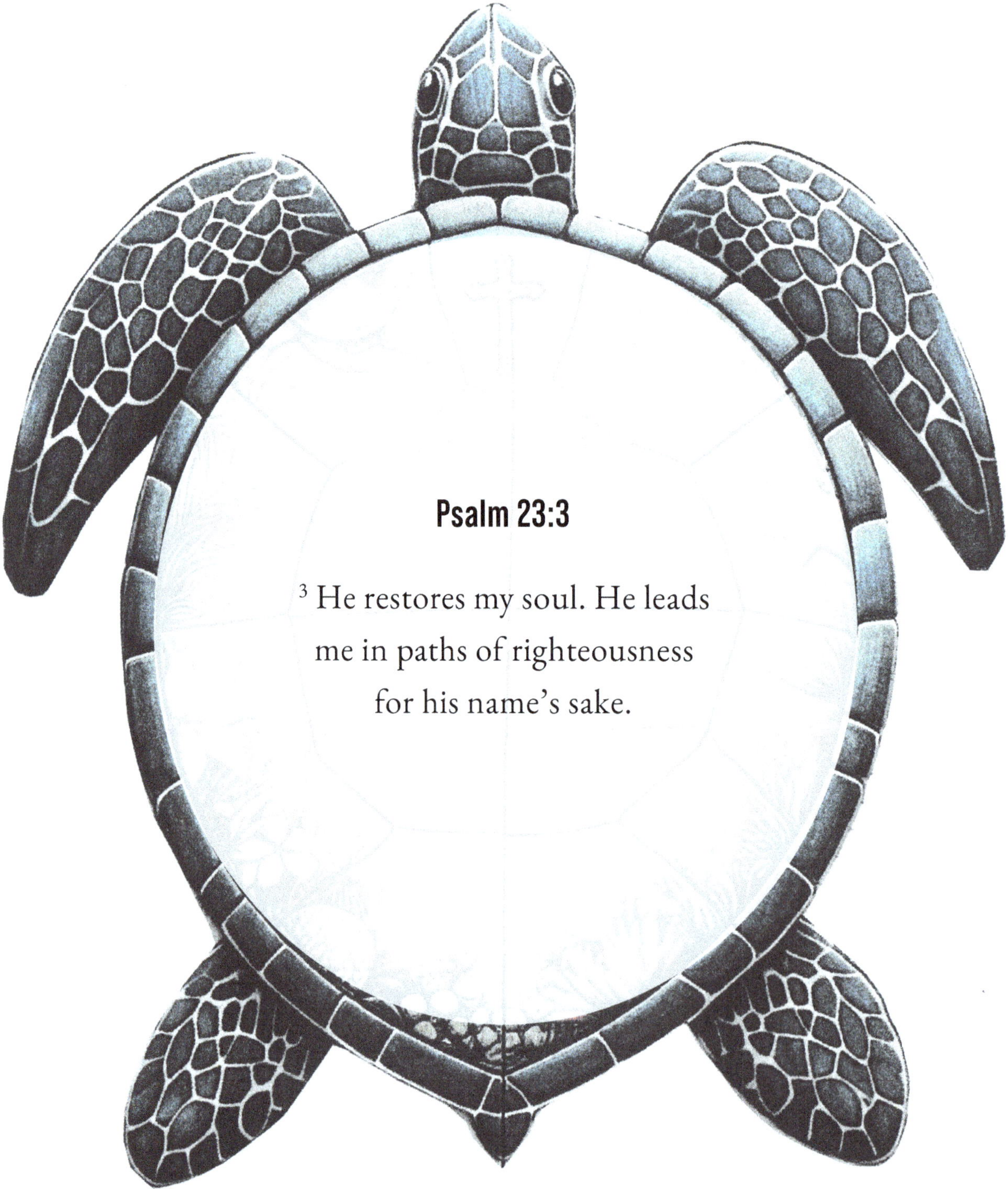

Psalm 23:3

3 He restores my soul. He leads
me in paths of righteousness
for his name's sake.

Reflection

How is being in a community of believers and followers of Jesus helped you on your faith journey?

_____
_____
_____
_____
_____
_____
_____
_____
_____
_____
_____
_____
_____

> Blessed are they who see beautiful things in humble places where other people see nothing.
>
> -Camille Pissarro

Gratitude

"Today I am thankful for the Pastors at my church, their messages are always timely and meaningful, helping to guide my next "right step"."

–Barbara

Being Grateful

Write down what you are grateful for today.

Date: _____

1. _____

   _____

   _____

2. _____

   _____

   _____

3. _____

   _____

   _____

Day Ten

Turtle Talk

Like a turtle can't turn its head to look backwards, don't worry about yesterday. The past is past, what is gone is gone. Focus on the here and now, the present.

Matthew 6:34

³⁴ "Therefore do not be anxious about tomorrow, for tomorrow will be anxious for itself. Sufficient for the day is its own trouble.

What do you need to say a final goodbye to?

> "Sometimes we should express our gratitude for the small and simple things like the scent of the rain, the taste of your favorite food, or the sound of a loved one's voice.
>
> -Joseph B. Worthlin"

Gratitude

"Today I am thankful for the many beautiful memories in my past, but I am also thankful for whatever lies ahead, I trust in His plan for my future."

–Barbara

Being Grateful

Write down what you are grateful for today.

Date: _____

1. _____
   _____
   _____

2. _____
   _____
   _____

3. _____
   _____
   _____

Day Eleven

Turtle Talk

Like a turtle, nature is slow, but sure, she works no faster than need be, she is the tortoise that wins the race by her perseverance. (Henry David Thoreau)

James 1:24

²⁴ For he looks at himself and goes away and at once forgets what he was like.

Reflection

When was the last time you recall preserving through an adversity?

_____
_____
_____
_____
_____
_____
_____
_____
_____
_____
_____
_____
_____
_____

> I am happy because I'm grateful. I choose to be grateful. That gratitude allows me to be happy.
>
> -Will Arnett

Gratitude

"Today I am thankful for my sister Kat, she has been "my person" through the most turbulent times of my life. She patiently listens and reminds me of God's promises letting me know it is okay to take one day at a time."

–Barbara

Being Grateful

Write down what you are grateful for today.

Date: _____

1. _____

   _____

   _____

2. _____

   _____

   _____

3. _____

   _____

   _____

Day Twelve

Turtle Talk

Like a turtle, try to be at ease in your own shell. (Bill Copeland)
Learn to love yourself (yep, all of you), right where you are.

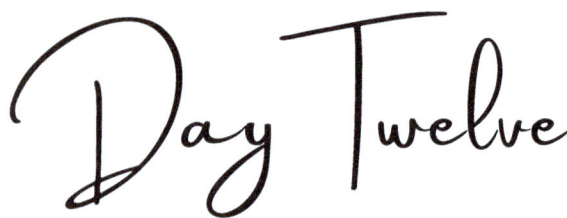

Psalm 139:13-15

¹³ For you formed my inward parts;
you knitted me together in my mother's womb.
¹⁴ I praise you, for I am fearfully
and wonderfully made.
Wonderful are your works;
my soul knows it very well.
¹⁵ My frame was not hidden from you,
when I was being made in secret,
intricately woven in the depths of the earth.

Reflection

How do you feel about yourself? What does it mean to you that were fearfully and wonderfully made? How does what God says about you change your perception of yourself?

_____

_____

_____

_____

_____

_____

_____

_____

_____

_____

_____

_____

> If you want to find happiness, find gratitude.
>
> -Steve Maraboli

Gratitude

"Today I am thankful to having a personal trainer, even if it is only for a short time. He taught me that I am strong and I am worthy, just as I am."

–Barbara

Being Grateful

Write down what you are grateful for today.

Date: _____

1. _____

   _____

   _____

2. _____

   _____

   _____

3. _____

   _____

   _____

Day Thirteen

Turtle Talk

Just like a sleepy turtle, you'll never catch up with the sunrise. (Jamaican proverb)
Don't sleep through your whole life, be present.

Philippians 4:6-7

Do not be anxious about anything, but in every situation, by prayer and petition, with thanksgiving, present your requests to God. And the peace of God, which transcends all understanding, will guard your hearts and your minds in Christ Jesus.

Reflection

What's a personal goal you can set based on this scripture?

_____
_____
_____
_____
_____
_____
_____
_____
_____
_____
_____
_____

> Sometimes the smallest things
> take up the most room in your heart.
>
> –Winnie the Pooh

Gratitude

"Today I am thankful for my brother Jeff. He often reminds me not to be anxious and that it is all going to be okay. He might not live close, but I know he'll always be there for me."

–Barbara

Being Grateful

Write down what you are grateful for today.

Date: _____

1. _____

   _____

   _____

2. _____

   _____

   _____

3. _____

   _____

   _____

Day Fourteen

Turtle Talk

Like a turtle navigates the currents, learn to ride life's highs and lows instead of struggling against them.

Romans 8:39

³⁹ nor height nor depth, nor anything else in all creation, will be able to separate us from the love of God in Christ Jesus our Lord.

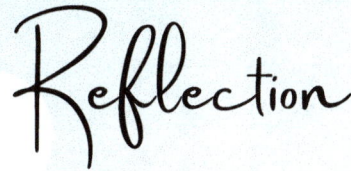

How would you help someone using this scripture during a stormy season?

_____
_____
_____
_____
_____
_____
_____
_____
_____
_____
_____
_____
_____

> "In life, one has a choice to take one of two paths: to wait for some special day or to celebrate each special day.
>
> –Rasheed Ogunlaru

Gratitude

"Today I am thankful for my soul sister Sherry. She has walked through the fire with me, helping me to navigate through a divorce while walking through her own and we've been riding the highs and lows of life together ever since."

–Barbara

Being Grateful

Write down what you are grateful for today.

Date: _____

1. _____
   _____
   _____

2. _____
   _____
   _____

3. _____
   _____
   _____

Day Fifteen

Turtle Talk

Like a turtle, become a skilled navigator. Chart your course, have a plan but remain flexible and open to God's guidance.

Nehemiah 9:12

¹² By a pillar of cloud you led them in the day, and by a pillar of fire in the night to light for them the way in which they should go.

Reflection

How has God been a pillar in your life?

> Gratitude and attitude are not challenges;
> they are choices.
>
> -Robert Braathe

Gratitude

"Today I am thankful for the free bible app "You Version". It has helped guide me and gotten me back into the bible each and every day."

–Barbara

Being Grateful

Write down what you are grateful for today.

Date: _____

1. _____

_____

_____

2. _____

_____

_____

3. _____

_____

_____

Day Sixteen

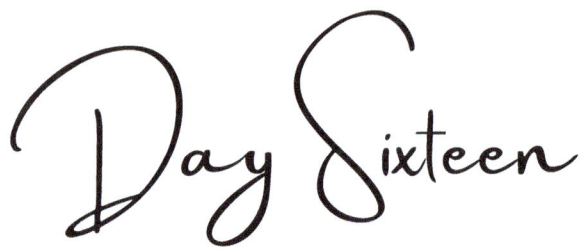

Turtle Talk

Like a turtle, sometimes you are digging yourself out of a hole you didn't dig.
Don't give up. Do not lose hope.

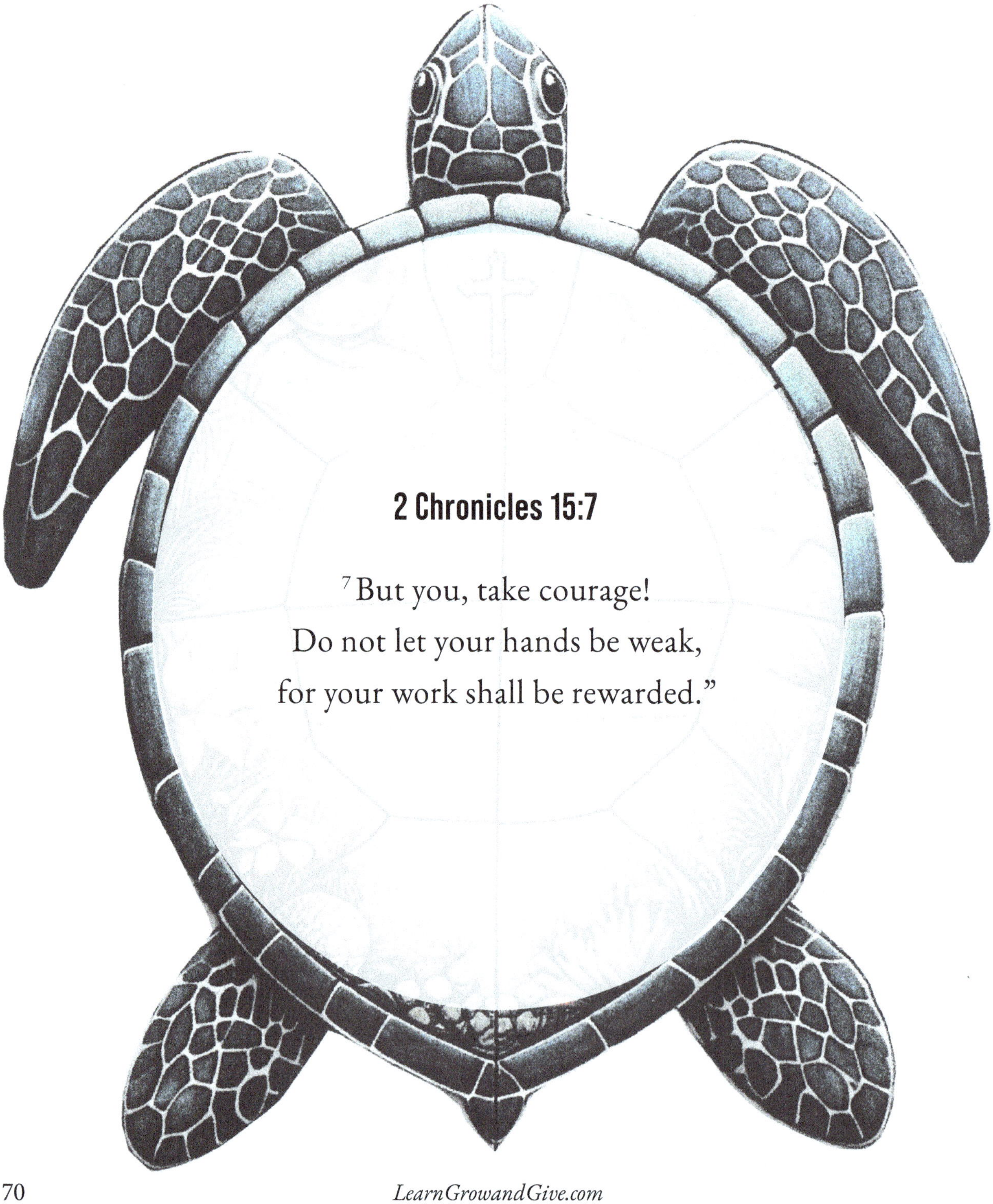

2 Chronicles 15:7

7 But you, take courage!
Do not let your hands be weak,
for your work shall be rewarded."

Reflection

What was the last miracle you recall in your life?

_____
_____
_____
_____
_____
_____
_____
_____
_____
_____
_____
_____
_____

> Enter his gates with thanksgiving and his courts with praise; give thanks to him and praise his name.
>
> –Psalms 100:4

Gratitude

"Today I am thankful for my friends Noreen and Lisa. They often reminded me to keep going, not to lose hope and that tomorrow is a new day."

–Barbara

Being Grateful

Write down what you are grateful for today.

Date: _____

1. _____
   _____
   _____

2. _____
   _____
   _____

3. _____
   _____
   _____

Day Seventeen

Turtle Talk

Like a turtle has a slower pace, this pace allows you to be present and to enjoy the beauty and miracles around you, made by God.

Phil 4:6

Do not be anxious about anything but in every situation, by prayer and petition, with thanksgiving, present your requests to God.

Reflection

What worries or anxieties can you surrender to God today through prayer, thanksgiving and trusting in His peace and provision?

> Come to me, all you who are weary and burdened, and I will give you rest. Take my yoke upon you and learn from me, for I am gentle and humble in heart, and you will find rest for your souls. For my yoke is easy and my burden is light.
>
> —Matthew 11:28-30

Gratitude

"Today I am thankful for my very cool cat, Mr. Simba. He reminds me to be in the present moment, to stop and relax, and to just BE! Who knew I was also a cat person?"

–Barbara

Being Grateful

Write down what you are grateful for today.

Date: _____

1. _____

_____

_____

2. _____

_____

_____

3. _____

_____

_____

Day Eighteen

Turtle Talk

Like a turtle, patience requires practice.
It takes time and opportunities to develop patience.

Romans 8:25

²⁵ But if we hope for what we do not see, we wait for it with patience.

Reflection

How have you had to practice patience recently?

_____
_____
_____
_____
_____
_____
_____
_____
_____
_____
_____
_____
_____

> Rejoice always.
>
> Thessalonians 5:16

Gratitude

"Today I am thankful for the year when I thought it was a good idea to pray for more patience. Be careful what you pray for. While it was a tough year, I was provided many opportunities to "practice" patience. You don't just get handed more, you get opportunities to practice it in order to have more of it."

–Barbara

Being Grateful

Write down what you are grateful for today.

Date: _____

1. _____

   _____

   _____

2. _____

   _____

   _____

3. _____

   _____

   _____

Day Nineteen

Turtle Talk

Like a turtle, you may not see or know where you are headed, but you keep moving forward, one turtle sized step at a time, moving forward in faith.

Proverbs 3:5-6

⁵ Trust in the Lord with all your heart,
and do not lean on your own understanding.
⁶ In all your ways acknowledge him,
and he will make straight your paths.

Reflection

If you were to live out this scripture every day, what changes would you need to make in your life?

> Give thanks in all circumstances;
> for this is God's will for you in Christ Jesus.
>
> -1 Thessalonians 5:18

Gratitude

"Today I am thankful for being able to be part of not one, but two Alpha classes. The curriculum reminded me about all the things I learned in Church and in youth group growing up in Minnesota. The people in both groups were so very supportive and loving as I was healing through the divorce process. I will be forever grateful for their kindness."

–Barbara

Being Grateful

Write down what you are grateful for today.

Date: _____

1. _____

   _____

   _____

2. _____

   _____

   _____

3. _____

   _____

   _____

Day Twenty

Turtle Talk

Like a turtle, eat only what you need to nourish your body. Turtles don't over eat or over indulge. Get healthy and stay healthy so you can be at your best to do what God has called you to do.

1 Corinthians 10:31

³¹ So whether you eat or drink
or whatever you do,
do it all for the glory of God.

Reflection

What actions are you inspired to take after reflecting on this scripture?

> Thanks be to God for his indescribable gift!
>
> -2 Cor 9:15

Gratitude

"Today I am thankful for the influence of my vegan friend and for the whole food/plant-based eating introduced to me by the owners of the Revelations Café."

–Barbara

Being Grateful

Write down what you are grateful for today.

Date: _____

1. _____

   _____

   _____

2. _____

   _____

   _____

3. _____

   _____

   _____

Day Twenty One

Turtle Talk

Like a turtle, its okay to have a hard shell for protection. Like the armor of God, another element is His shield of faith, put it on to protect yourself.

Ephesians 6:10-18

The Armor of God

¹⁰ Finally, be strong in the Lord and in his mighty power. ¹¹ Put on the full armor of God, so that you can take your stand against the devil's schemes. ¹² For our struggle is not against flesh and blood, but against the rulers, against the authorities, against the powers of this dark world and against the spiritual forces of evil in the heavenly realms. ¹³ Therefore put on the full armor of God, so that when the day of evil comes, you may be able to stand your ground, and after you have done everything, to stand. ¹⁴ Stand firm then, with the belt of truth buckled around your waist, with the breastplate of righteousness in place, ¹⁵ and with your feet fitted with the readiness that comes from the gospel of peace. ¹⁶ In addition to all this, take up the shield of faith, with which you can extinguish all the flaming arrows of the evil one. ¹⁷ Take the helmet of salvation and the sword of the Spirit, which is the word of God. ¹⁸ And pray in the Spirit on all occasions with all kinds of prayers and requests. With this in mind, be alert and always keep on praying for all the Lord's people.

How has God protected you in the past? How have you used the Armor of God in your daily life?

_____
_____
_____
_____
_____
_____
_____
_____
_____
_____
_____
_____
_____

> Give thanks to the Lord, for he is good;
> his love endures forever.
>
> -1 Chron 16:34

Gratitude

"Today I am thankful the guidance and support from my counselor. She reminded me often of how strong I am and to lean on my faith. Yes, it is okay to go to counseling. I highly recommend seeking out support from a certified counselor during the tough seasons of your life to help navigate those waters and chart a course towards healing."

–Barbara

Being Grateful

Write down what you are grateful for today.

Date: _____

1. _____
   _____
   _____

2. _____
   _____
   _____

3. _____
   _____
   _____

Day Twenty Two

Turtle Talk

Like a turtle, while you may have put up a shell around you for protection, do not let it harden your heart.

1 Peter 3:8-9

⁸ Finally, all of you, have unity of mind, sympathy, brotherly love, a tender heart, and a humble mind. ⁹ Do not repay evil for evil or reviling for reviling, but on the contrary, bless, for to this you were called, that you may obtain a blessing.

How has God helped you have a tender heart?

> Now our God, we give you thanks,
> and praise your glorious name.
>
> -1 Chron 29:13

Gratitude

"Today I am thankful for all of my sisters. Yes, I have a few, more than most have. I have been blessed with seven sisters. While one has passed away, the other six were so very supportive during the toughest season of my life. They sent me cards of encouragement, talked and listened to me on the phone when I needed it, and helped me move. I will be forever grateful for their love, support, guidance, grace, and prayers."

–Barbara

Being Grateful

Write down what you are grateful for today.

Date: _____

1. _____

   _____

   _____

2. _____

   _____

   _____

3. _____

   _____

   _____

Day Twenty Three

Turtle Talk

Like a turtle uses her tail to steer in the direction she's swimming, remember to use God's words to guide your steps.

Psalm 37:23-24

²³ The steps of a man are
established by the Lord,
when he delights in his way;
²⁴ though he fall, he shall not be cast headlong,
for the Lord upholds his hand.

Reflection

How had God guided your steps?

_____
_____
_____
_____
_____
_____
_____
_____
_____
_____
_____
_____

> I will praise God's name in song
> and glorify him with thanksgiving.
>
> -Psalms 69:30

Gratitude

"Today I am thankful for the Connect Groups and classes at my church. They helped keep me in God's word and walk out my faith with other Christians trying to do the same. Remember, we are not meant to walk through life alone, we were designed to be in community."

–Barbara

Being Grateful

Write down what you are grateful for today.

Date: _____

1. _____

   _____

   _____

2. _____

   _____

   _____

3. _____

   _____

   _____

Day Twenty Four

Turtle Talk

Like a turtle comes in all shapes and sizes, so do we.
Learn to love your body as it is right now and for the temple it is.

1 Corinthians 6:19-20

¹⁹ Or do you not know that your body is a temple of the Holy Spirit within you, whom you have from God? You are not your own, ²⁰ for you were bought with a price. So glorify God in your body.

Reflection

What are your thoughts or feelings about your own body image in relation to this idea? How does that line up to what God says about you?

_____
_____
_____
_____
_____
_____
_____
_____
_____
_____
_____

> Let us come into his presence with thanksgiving;
> let us make a joyful noise to him with songs of praise.
>
> –Psalm 95:2

Gratitude

"Today I am thankful for giving myself grace when I don't practice healthy eating habits or don't take that daily walk. I will continue to try my best and pray for more self-control and discipline to treat my body in a way that will help me do what He has called me to do."

–Barbara

Being Grateful

Write down what you are grateful for today.

Date: _____

1. _____

   _____

   _____

2. _____

   _____

   _____

3. _____

   _____

   _____

Day Twenty Five

Turtle Talk

Like a turtle, don't worry about what you'll wear or eat.
God promises to provide for all your needs.

Phil 4:19

¹⁹ And my God will supply every need of yours according to his riches in glory in Christ Jesus.

Reflection

In what ways has God met your needs?

Every good gift and every perfect gift is from above, coming down from the Father of lights, with whom there is no variation or shadow due to change.

-James 1:17

Gratitude

"Today I am thankful for my career and having one that empowers me to serve others and inspire growth through coaching."

–Barbara

Being Grateful

Write down what you are grateful for today.

Date: _____

1. _____
   _____
   _____
   _____

2. _____
   _____
   _____
   _____

3. _____
   _____
   _____
   _____

Day Twenty Six

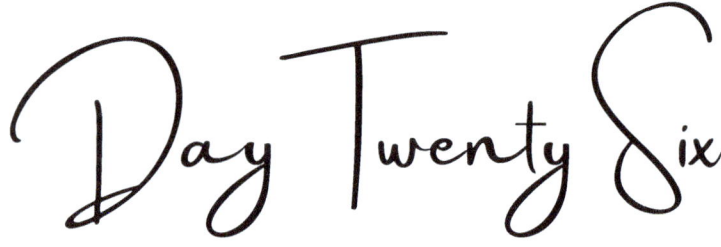

Turtle Talk

Like a turtle, be confident in your identity, which is a child of God. Your true identity is not in being a wife, a mother, a sister, or the title on your business card. Those are roles God has given you to fulfill your purpose.

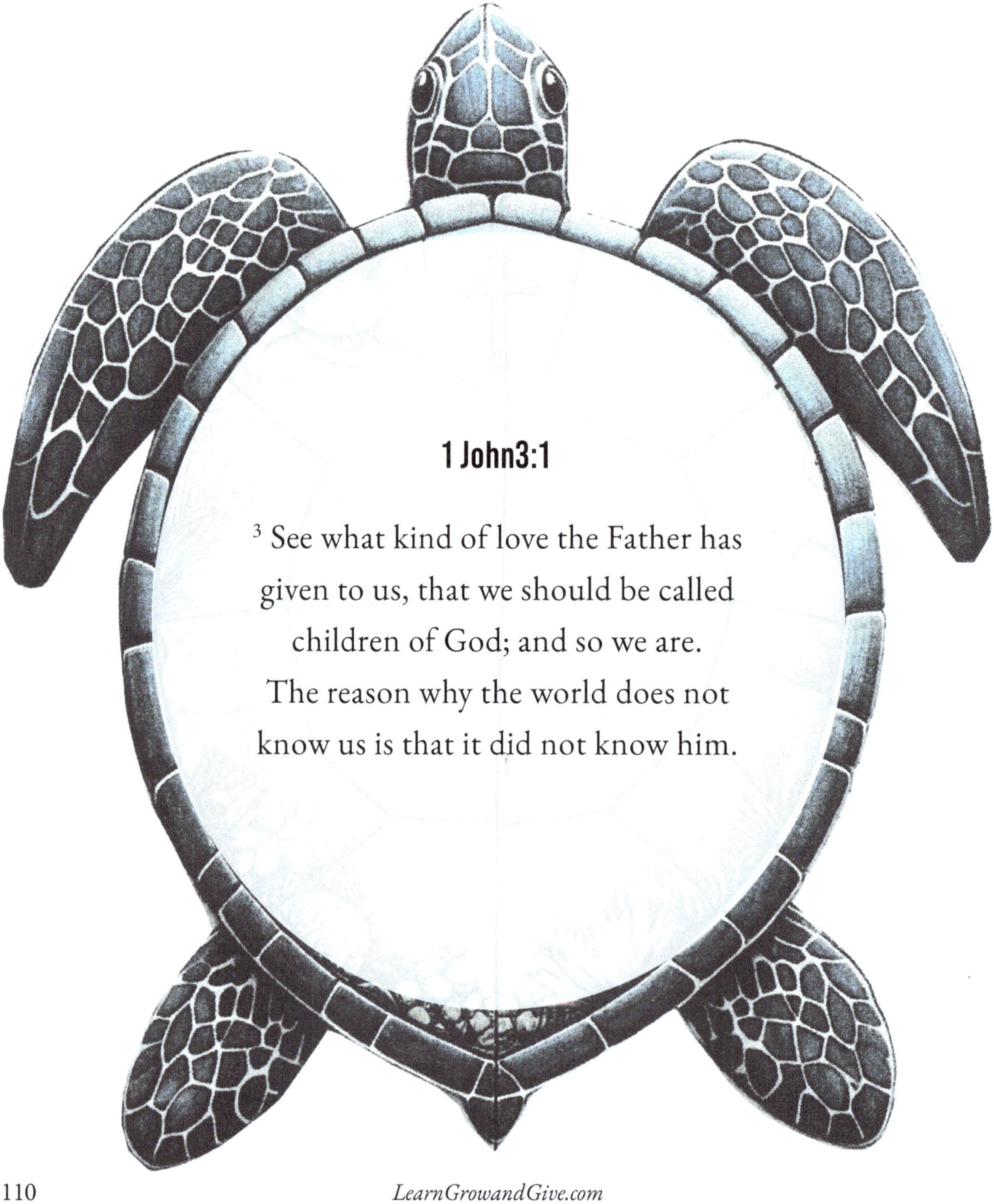

1 John3:1

3 See what kind of love the Father has given to us, that we should be called children of God; and so we are. The reason why the world does not know us is that it did not know him.

How does understanding your identity in Christ shape the way you view yourself and others in your daily life?

> Oh, give thanks to the Lord; call upon his name;
> make known his deeds among the peoples!
>
> -Psalms 105:1

Gratitude

"I am deeply thankful for finally realizing my true identity. As a child of God, I am His cherished daughter."

–Barbara

Being Grateful

Write down what you are grateful for today.

Date: _____

1. _____
   _____
   _____

2. _____
   _____
   _____

3. _____
   _____
   _____

Day Twenty Seven

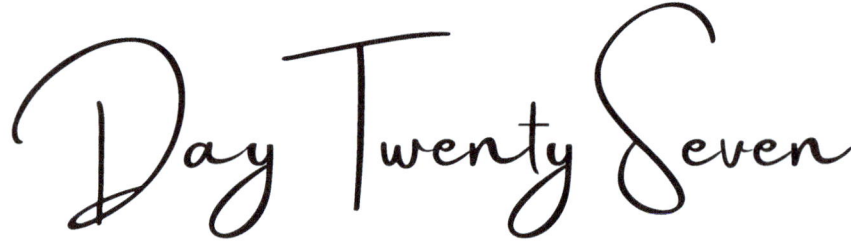

Turtle Talk

Like a turtle swims to higher ground in stormy weather,
when life's storms come, lean into your faith.

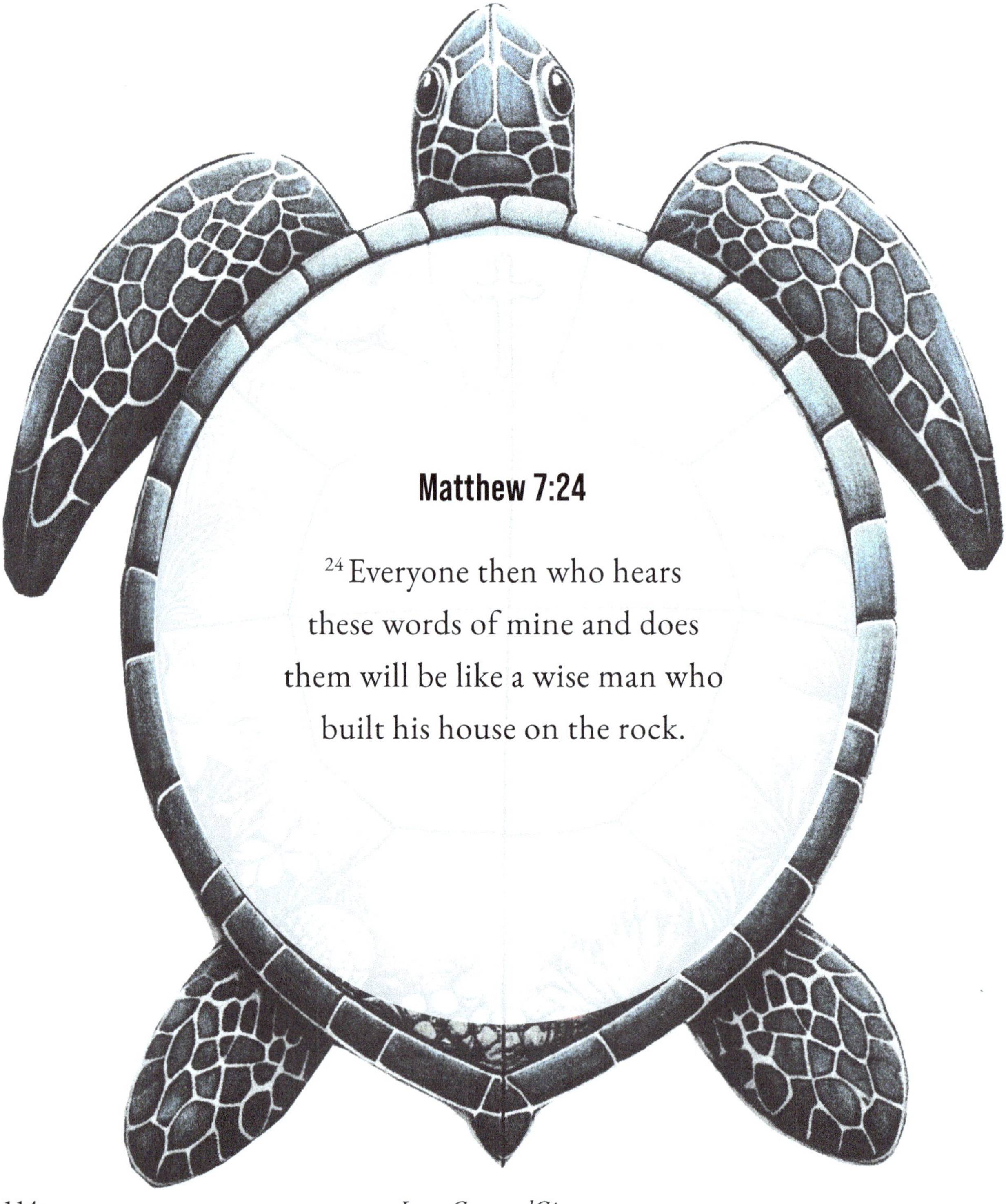

Matthew 7:24

[24] Everyone then who hears these words of mine and does them will be like a wise man who built his house on the rock.

Reflection

What scriptures have helped you weather life's storms?

> "I will give thanks to the Lord with my whole heart;
> I will recount all of your wonderful deeds.
>
> –Psalm 9:1

Gratitude

"Today I am very thankful to call Kelly and Mike my friends. They were there for me through the past twenty plus years and to be their next door neighbor once again is truly a blessing!"

–Barbara

Being Grateful

Write down what you are grateful for today.

Date: _____

1. _____

   _____

   _____

2. _____

   _____

   _____

3. _____

   _____

   _____

Day Twenty Eight

Turtle Talk

Like a turtle crosses the road carefully, be deliberate and careful in making big decisions. Pray about them, ask for discernment.

Psalm 32:8

⁸ I will instruct you and teach you in the way you should go; I will counsel you with my loving eye on you.

Reflection

In what areas of your life do you feel uncertain or confused, and how can you seek God's wisdom and discernment to guide your decisions in those areas?

_____
_____
_____
_____
_____
_____
_____
_____
_____
_____
_____

> And let the peace of Christ rule in your hearts, to which indeed you were called in one body. And be thankful.
>
> -Colossians 3:15

Gratitude

"Today I am thankful for God providing me guidance over the years when making big life altering decisions. They aren't always easy, but eventually you can see the "why" behind the struggle."

–Barbara

Being Grateful

Write down what you are grateful for today.

Date: _____

1. _____
   _____
   _____

2. _____
   _____
   _____

3. _____
   _____
   _____

Day Twenty Nine

Turtle Talk

Like a turtle, don't live your life in fear.
Learn to put all of your fears in God's hands and trust in Him.

Psalm 34:4

⁴ I sought the Lord, and he answered me;
he delivered me from all my fears.

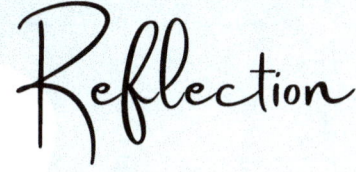

What challenges have you faced that have made it difficult to trust God's plans, and how might those experiences be shaping your faith and understanding of His purpose for your life?

> Be grateful, kind and joyful, each and every day.
>
> -Barbara Kleinsorge

Gratitude

"Today I am thankful for growing so much in my faith that I no longer live from a place of fear or regret. I remember God's Five Finger Promise: I will never leave thee. I trust in His plan for my life. He's got me in His the palm of His Hands."

–Barbara

Being Grateful

Write down what you are grateful for today.

Date: _____

1. _____
   _____
   _____

2. _____
   _____
   _____

3. _____
   _____
   _____

Day Thirty

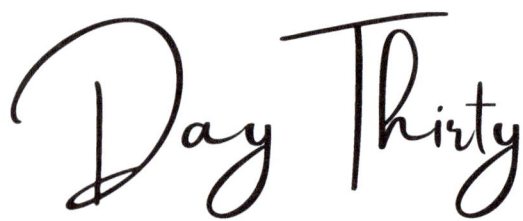

Turtle Talk

Like a turtle can't move forward without sticking her neck out,
we can't move forward without taking a step out in faith.

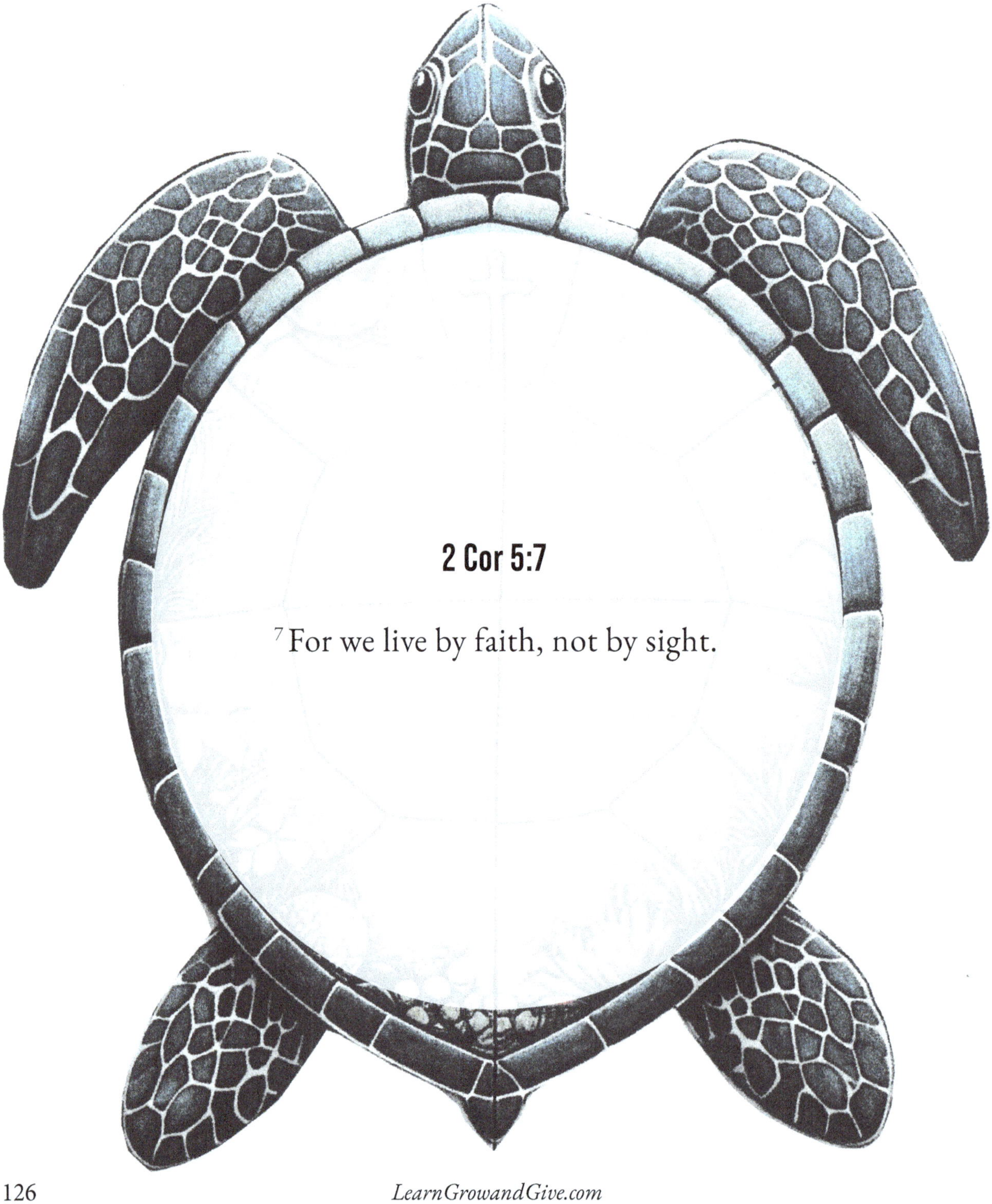

2 Cor 5:7

7 For we live by faith, not by sight.

Reflection

In what areas of your life is God asking you to trust Him more fully?

> God, I cannot begin to express my gratitude
> for your countless blessings in my life.
>
> —Barbara Kleinsorge

Gratitude

"Today I am thankful for my "Grow Life" coach, teacher and friend, Cynda. Over the past ten plus years, she has ever so patiently been helping me move my story forward, to slowly crawl out of my shell again and to step out in faith and obedience."

–Barbara

Being Grateful

Write down what you are grateful for today.

Date: _____

1. _____

_____

_____

2. _____

_____

_____

3. _____

_____

_____

Day Thirty One

Turtle Talk

Like a turtle's neck doesn't allow for it to look behind her, don't look backwards, you aren't going that direction. Learn the lessons from the past so you don't repeat them, but look forward towards your future, stronger because of your past.

Genesis 19:26

⁶ But Lot's wife, behind him, looked back, and she became a pillar of salt.

Jeremiah 29:11

¹¹ For I know the plans I have for you, declares the Lord, plans for welfare and not for evil, to give you a future and a hope.

Reflection

In what areas of your life are you tempted to look back at? How might God be calling you to let go and move forward in faith, trusting in His plan for your future?

> Learn God, grow in faith, and give love.
>
> –Barbara Kleinsorge

Gratitude

"Today I am thankful my family and friends who have often reminded me to keep looking forward and not to the past. I am grateful for today and I am excited about the promise of tomorrow."

–Barbara

Being Grateful

Write down what you are grateful for today.

Date: _____

1. _____

   _____

   _____

2. _____

   _____

   _____

3. _____

   _____

   _____

Epilogue

You made it! Congratulations! I am proud of you! As this time of Turtle Talk with God comes to a close, let's take a moment to reflect on the key themes we've explored. We dug into what it means to praise God during our stormy seasons of life, those seasons where we are waiting on Him. His timing isn't always our timing. Throughout this journey together, we've delved into the depth of the similarities of turtles and our own walk of faith, discovering how they apply to our daily lives. I am thankful for finding joy and peace again through my faith and trust in His promises and know that is possible for you.

It is my hope that these reflections have inspired you and provided you with reminders of God's promises for you and that He has you, and is with you through all seasons of your life. Each day presents us with an opportunity to learn, grow and give to others. How you start and end your day determines what kind of life you live. I pray that this daily practice of reading God's word and practicing gratitude has helped you in your faith journey. I hope you join me again as we continue this journey into a new season of joy, peace and restoration in my next devotional... until then, walk out your faith every day, even if it's a turtle sized step. Blessings!

Learn, Grow and Give is dedicated to helping women and girls discover their true identities, strengths and purposes.

LearnGrowandGive.com

Barbara's Bio

About The Author

Barbara, age 60, is the twelfth of fourteen children, raised in the heart of the Midwest, where family bonds and resilience were forged early on. With a deep understanding of life's challenges, including the joys and trials of having two brothers with Down Syndrome, she has cultivated a unique perspective that influences her storytelling and empathy for those in need.

After moving to Florida right after high school, Barbara began a journey that would see her marry at 21, raise three beautiful children, and become a grandmother to two adorable grandchildren. She is currently in her 34-year career in education—where she progressed from teacher to principal and currently serves as a supervisor for the county's homeless program. She blends her professional insights with her personal narrative to empower others through her life coaching business.

Recently, she launched her Christian life coaching business, **_Learn, Grow and Give_**, dedicated to helping women and girls discover their true identities, strengths and purposes. As the President of Pasco's Alpha Delta Kappa (ADK) and Chaplain for District V ADK, she is passionately involved in her community. She also serves on the Coalition for the Homeless of Pasco County's Leadership Council working to provide assistance to those in need.

In her role as an Usher and Connect Group leader at theChapel, she fosters connections and community, embodying her belief in the power of service, hospitality, and compassion. With a heart full of stories to tell and a mission to inspire, Barbara invites her readers to join her on this journey of faith, growth, resilience, and discovery.

www.ingramcontent.com/pod-product-compliance
Lightning Source LLC
Chambersburg PA
CBHW080437230426
43662CB00015B/2297